A Number Scavenger Hunt

by Kerry Dinmont

The Child's World®
childsworld.com

Published by The Child's World®
1980 Lookout Drive • Mankato, MN 56003-1705
800-599-READ • www.childsworld.com

ISBN 9781503823631
LCCN 2017944882

Printed in the United States of America
PA02361

About the Author

Kerry Dinmont is a children's book
author who enjoys art and nature.
She lives in Montana with her two
Norwegian elkhounds.

We use numbers every day. Numbers help us count things. Turn the page to see if you can find the different numbers in this book!

We count with numbers. The number "one" stands for a single thing, such as a dog. If there are many dogs, we say numbers in order, beginning with one. When we have given a number to the last dog, we have counted the number of dogs.

How many dogs can you count in this picture?

Some numbers are even numbers. They can be split into **sets** of two. For example, the number four can be split into two sets of two.

Which vase has an even number of flowers?

Other numbers are odd numbers. When split into sets of two, one number will always be by itself. The number five can be split into two sets of two and one by itself.

Which bowls have an odd number of fruit?

Zero is a number. It stands for no **countable** things. A table that has no plates on it has zero plates.

Which basket has zero kittens in it?

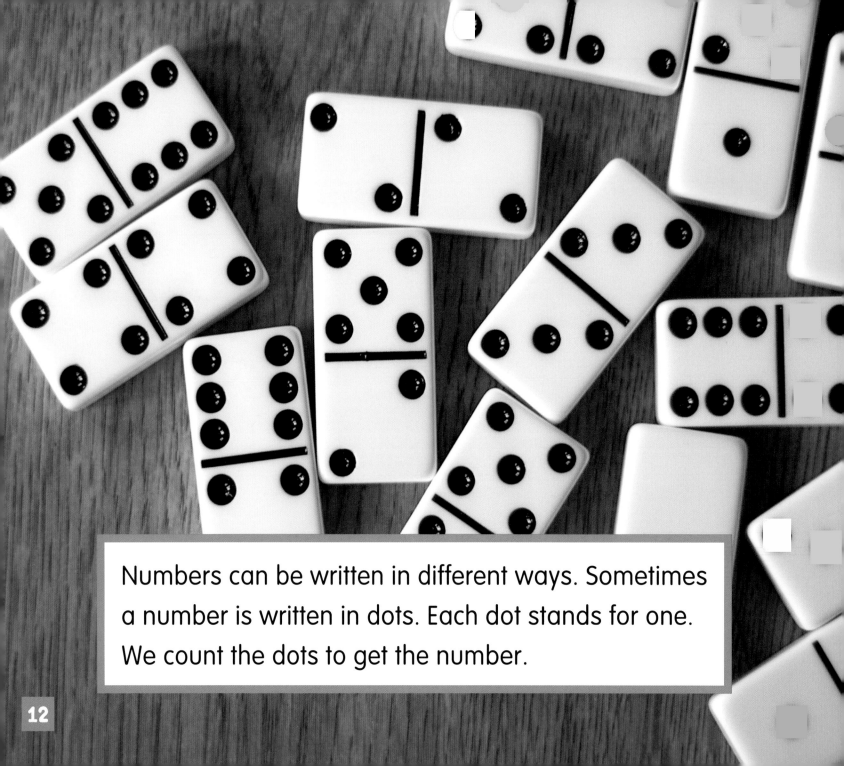

Numbers can be written in different ways. Sometimes a number is written in dots. Each dot stands for one. We count the dots to get the number.

Which of these dice shows the number five?

We use Arabic **numerals**. The numerals 0 through 9 came from **ancient** India. Numbers can also be written as Roman numerals. These numbers came from ancient Rome. An "I" stands for one. "V" stands for five. "X" stands for ten.

Which of these clocks has the Roman numeral for ten?

Two numbers can combine to make a bigger number. This is called **addition**. The bigger number is the **sum**. For example, you might have two blue shoes and two pink shoes. The sum is four shoes.

Which group of jellybeans adds up to six?

One number can be taken away from a larger number. This is called **subtraction**. For example, you might bake nine cookies. But you eat one of them. This leaves you with eight cookies.

Which group of eggs has one less egg than the others?

Numbers are everywhere. They help us stay organized.

How many numbers can you find in this football game?

Answer Key

Page 5   **How many dogs can you count in this picture?** There are three dogs in this picture.

Page 7   **Which vase has an even number of flowers?** The clear vase has four flowers, which is an even number.

Page 9   **Which bowls have an odd number of fruit?** The bowl of strawberries has seven pieces of fruit, and the bowl of green apples has three pieces of fruit. Both are odd numbers.

Page 11   **Which basket has zero kittens in it?** The basket with a single handle has zero kittens.

Page 13   **Which of these dice shows the number five?** The die in the upper right-hand corner shows the number five.

Page 15   **Which of these clocks has the Roman numeral for ten?** The brown clock has the Roman numeral for ten.

Page 17   **Which group of jellybeans adds up to six?** The group of red jellybeans adds up to six.

Page 19   **Which group of eggs has one less egg than the others?** The group of white eggs has two eggs. It has one less egg than the other groups. The other groups of eggs each have three eggs.

Glossary

addition (uh-DISH-uhn) Addition is a calculation in which you add two or more numbers. Addition helps people add together groups of things, such as shoes.

ancient (AYN-shunt) Something that is ancient is old or comes from the past. Arabic numerals come from ancient India.

countable (KOWNT-uh-buhl) Something that is countable can be counted. The number zero stands for no countable things.

numerals (NEW-mur-uhlz) Numerals are written symbols that stand for numbers. Some numbers are written as Roman numerals.

sets (SETZ) Sets are groups of things. Even numbers can be split into sets of two.

subtraction (suhb-TRAK-shun) Subtraction is a calculation in which you take away a smaller number from a larger number. Subtraction helps people find out how many things were taken away or how many things are left.

To Learn More

Books

Browne, Anthony. *One Gorilla: A Counting Book.* Somerville, MA: Candlewick Press, 2013.

Pistoia, Sara. *Counting.* Mankato, MN: The Child's World, 2014.

Schuh, Mari. *The Crayola Counting Book.* Minneapolis, MN: Lerner Publications, 2018.

Web Sites

Visit our Web site for links about numbers and counting:
childsworld.com/links

Note to Parents, Teachers, and Librarians: We routinely verify our Web links to make sure they are safe and active sites. So encourage your readers to check them out!